NO NEED

TO

PANIC

A Guide to Managing and Overcoming Panic Attacks

By

Jerry B. Olsen

Table of Contents

Introduction

If you're reading this book, chances are you or a loved one has experienced the terrible and overpowering symptoms of a panic attack. Panic episodes may be upsetting and unpleasant, negatively influencing quality of life. The good news is that panic episodes can be controlled and treated.

This book examines panic attacks, why they happen, and how to manage and conquer them successfully. We will look at several tactics and approaches for dealing with panic episodes, challenging negative thought patterns, and building resilience. We will also go through lifestyle modifications, pharmaceutical alternatives, and the significance of self-care in the healing process.

Additionally, this book intends to help you flourish in the face of panic episodes rather than merely manage them. You will discover techniques for avoiding relapse, living stress-free and fostering mindfulness and emotional well-being. You will also learn practical activities that will help you on your path to health.

Understand that you are not alone and that there is still hope. We will investigate techniques to manage, conquer, and eventually flourish beyond panic episodes. Therefore, let us plunge in and begin our journey toward a life free of anxiety.

Chapter 1

Understanding Panic Attacks,

What exactly is a panic attack?

A panic attack is a brief and acute period of worry caused by a perceived or genuine threat. It elicits an overwhelming reaction in your body.

Panic attack symptoms can occur for various reasons and do not always indicate a mental health problem.

A panic attack may happen to anyone. Yet, some people who suffer panic episodes and are constantly worried about getting them might develop panic disorder. Yet, not everyone who suffers from panic episodes has panic disorder.

During a panic attack, you may simultaneously feel mental, physical, emotional, and cognitive symptoms.

The suddenness and severity of a panic attack can be frightening, prompting some individuals to feel they are having a heart attack or are in danger. You may feel weary and wobbly as a result of this.

Panic episodes are classified into two types: unexpected and expected. They are characterized in this manner based on the trigger and onset. Yet, the symptoms of both categories might be the same.

Unexpected Panic Attacks

There is no apparent reason or trigger for unexpected panic episodes. This implies it will take time to determine what caused your attack.

For example, you could be listening to music on the floor when you suddenly have a panic attack. You'd describe this as an unexpected panic attack because you are relaxed and rested.

A sudden panic attack might occur when sleeping, among friends, or eating at your favorite restaurant.

This isn't to say there isn't a trigger; it's just that identifying it is difficult.

The precise etiology of sudden panic episodes is unknown. Your brain may be picking up on environmental cues before your conscious self. That might be subliminal links to instances when you were afraid.

For example, a song, lighting effect, or perfume may cause your brain to associate the current moment with the last time you felt pain or fear. This might cause you to have a panic attack without you recognizing it.

In other circumstances, worry causes a panic attack.

Assume you've been stressed out recently and are worried about losing your job. You decide to do some gardening today to unwind. Instead, your heart begins to race, and you become dizzy. You are quickly concerned about these symptoms, which create new sensations. You get a sudden panic attack.

What causes a panic attack for you may be

completely different from what causes a panic attack for someone else. Most people discover that they have many triggers.

Sudden panic episodes can catch you off guard, causing even more worry and stress.

Panic disorder is typically diagnosed when you experience sudden panic attacks.

Expected Panic Attacks

Panic attacks are expected to occur due to a specifically identified cause.

For example, if you are frightened of confined places and are trapped in an elevator, you may experience an expected panic attack. If you've been worrying about having a medical operation, you might experience a panic attack while waiting.

In other words, you understand why you're worried.

Panic episodes can be either situational or

predisposed.

A situationally cued panic attack may occur soon after exposure to a specific context that has previously caused anxiety or panic attacks.

For instance, if you are afraid of spiders and come into touch with one, you may have a cued panic episode.

In contrast, a predisposed panic attack does not usually occur on cue after being exposed to the event.

For example, you may be frightened of flying but does not experience panic attacks every time you board a plane. Alternatively, you may experience panic before boarding, boarding, or exiting the plane.

You may also get a panic attack due to terrifying thoughts or worry.

Can a panic attack kill you?

Panic attack symptoms can be pretty overpowering. If your heart is beating, you're having difficulties breathing, and your mind is telling you that you're dying, it's easy to convince yourself that you're dying.

Experiencing this feeling during a panic attack is expected. Yet that is not what is occurring.

The adrenaline surge and hyperventilating cause heart palpitations, choking sensations, and lightheadedness during a panic attack. This and your racing thoughts might result in even more severe physical sensations.

While you may appear to be suffering a heart attack or a life-threatening encounter, you are not. In truth, panic attacks are rarely severe or fatal.

A rare exception would be if you fainted and banged your head or if your fear caused you to behave in a way that put you in grave danger. For example, suppose you were terrified and hurried out of your house, crossing the street without first looking for automobiles.

Nonetheless, these are relatively unusual events. During a panic episode, most people do not faint or run.

While panic attacks are seldom fatal, numerous episodes may impact your long-term health, especially if you have an underlying cardiovascular illness.

This is not to say that you can die from a panic attack, but it does suggest that having numerous episodes might increase your chance of developing certain health disorders.

This is why it is critical to seek expert assistance to avoid and control panic attack symptoms. It is also a good idea to practice relaxation methods regularly.

Symptoms of a Panic Attack

A panic attack is a short moment of intense anxiety accompanied by an excessive physiological response to a real or imagined threat or danger.

This unexpected burst of intense dread or anxiety causes physical and psychological consequences. They frequently reach their maximal intensity in a few minutes.

Panic episodes may be a one-time occurrence for many people. Some may experience it regularly. This is most common in the setting of a mental health issue such as panic disorder.

Yet, panic episodes are always treatable.

The first step in controlling panic attack symptoms, whether sporadic or regular, is to recognize what they are and how they feel.

The indications and symptoms of a panic attack appear suddenly and generally peak within 10 minutes. These seldom last more than an hour; the majorities are over in 20 to 30 minutes. Panic attacks can occur at any moment and in any place. You may have one while shopping, going down the street, driving your car, or even sitting on your couch at home.

Symptoms

1. Palpitations in the heart
2. Sweating
3. Tremors or shaking
4. Lack of breath or a sense of being suffocated
5. The sensation of choking
6. Chest discomfort
7. Nausea or stomach pain
8. feeling dizzy or lightheaded
9. Depersonalization or derealization
10. Anxiety over losing control or dying
11. Tingling or numbness
12. Cold sweats or hot flashes

A beating heart and palpitations

A frequent sign of panic episodes is a sudden increase in heart rate. You may feel or hear your heart pounding quicker or harder or notice a pulse point throbbing unusually loudly.

Once the panic attack and symptoms pass, your heart rate should decrease.

Sweating

Sweating may occur as part of the panic reaction. This can be uncomfortable or embarrassing if you're in public, but it usually only lasts a few minutes and is entirely natural.

Shaking or trembling

Excessive and uncontrollable trembling, or shaking in your hands and legs, is one of the earliest indications of a panic attack.

You may continue to shake albeit less strongly hours after your other panic attack symptoms have subsided. When you recuperate and calm down, the trembling should reduce.

While unpleasant, this panic attack symptom typically does not signal a medical condition.

Suffocating feelings and shortness of breath

Many individuals hyperventilate or feel as if they are suffocating during a panic attack. You may cough, gag, or even vomit because of this.

As powerful and unpleasant as these sensations may seem, they are a natural reaction to your adrenaline surge.

Concentrate on keeping your breathing constant by taking deep breaths in and out. During 5 to 30 minutes, your regular breathing rate should resume.

Choking sensation

Similar to shortness of breath, feeling like you're choking can be caused by hyperventilation. Panic attacks can be exacerbated by gasping for oxygen.

As difficult as it may be to recall during a panic attack, remember that this is a result of worry, not a medical ailment, you are not choking.

Pain or discomfort in the chest

Anxiety and chest discomfort may accompany heart palpitations and hyperventilation. The first time this happens is frequently frightening because you may mistake it for your heart and not understand its anxiety.

Although chest discomfort is a frequent panic attack symptom, it is critical to get medical attention if you have never had chest pain before. This can assist you in excluding any underlying heart problems.

A doctor can do tests and ask questions to determine if the problem is heart-related or anxiety-related.

Nausea or stomach pain

Nausea or stomach ache is another side effect of

all that adrenaline. These symptoms may intensify immediately during the height of the panic attack during the first 10 minutes.

You may feel sick for several hours after the attack has ended. Anxiety can induce stomach trouble in general.

Dizziness, unsteadiness, lightheadedness, or fainting

The combination of panic attack symptoms racing heart, hyperventilating, and dread of losing control can cause dizziness or lightheadedness.

This is a natural reaction to fear. Once the other symptoms have subsided, you should feel more stable.

Depersonalization or derealization

When panic attack symptoms worsen, you may suspect what's occurring isn't authentic or begin to perceive your surroundings differently, as if you're in a movie. This is known as derealization.

You may also experience a sense of disconnection from yourself as if you are not linked to your own body. This is known as depersonalization.

Concern about losing control

If this is your first panic attack, the acute sensations may make you feel you're losing control or your hold on reality. You may also get the sense that everything is closing in on you.

They are only fleeting sentiments, the result of all the physiological processes in your body, and do not reflect your mental health.

The fear of dying

One of the most prevalent symptoms of a panic attack is fear of death, especially in early episodes or those who rarely suffer panic attacks.

You may become concerned about your safety due to the physical symptoms and acute anxiety. Yet, while these sensations directly result from fear, they do not always suggest a medical or life-threatening condition.

Feelings of numbness or tingling

Anxiety and adrenaline may cause a pins-and-needles sensation to spread throughout your body.

You may also experience numbness or be temporarily frozen. These sensations usually pass after a few minutes.

Feelings of chills or heat

You may have chills or hot flashes in addition to heavy perspiration. This is your body's attempt to adjust to the adrenaline and terror rush.

Additional signs and experiences of a panic attack.

Other symptoms, such as weeping, headaches, or vomiting, may occur. But, to be diagnosed with a panic attack, you must exhibit at least four of the symptoms listed above.

A panic attack versus a meltdowns

A panic episode might take up to three days to completely recover from. Conversely, meltdowns occur as a result of the individual gradually becoming more stressed or nervous. These circumstances compound until the person has a nervous breakdown.

Is it a panic attack or a heart attack?

The majority of panic attack symptoms are physical, and they might be so severe that you worry you will have a heart attack. Many people who suffer from panic attacks visit the doctor or the emergency department several times to obtain care for what they fear is a life-threatening medical illness. While it's critical to rule out medical causes of symptoms like chest discomfort, an accelerated heart rate, or difficulty breathing, it's typically fear that gets missed as a probable cause, not the other way around.

Panic disorder signs and symptoms

While many individuals experience one or two panic attacks with no subsequent episodes or complications and there's no reason to worry if this is you, some people develop panic disorder. Panic disorder is characterized by recurring panic episodes and substantial behavioral changes or chronic concern about having more attacks. These signs and symptoms include:

• Having frequent, sudden panic episodes that aren't related to a specific situation.

• Worrying a lot about having another panic attack.

• Behaving differently as a result of the panic attacks, such as avoiding areas where you've previously panicked.

While a panic attack may only last a few minutes, the ramifications of the encounter might have long-term consequences. Recurrent panic episodes can be emotionally draining if you have a panic disorder. Recollecting the great anxiety and horror you felt during the assaults might harm your self-confidence and create significant disruption in your daily life. This eventually results in the following panic disorder symptoms:

Anticipatory anxiety - You feel worried and tense in between panic episodes instead of comfortable and like yourself. This anxiety is caused by a dread of having another panic attack. Most of the time, this "fear of dread" is there, and it can be pretty crippling.

Avoidance of phobic situations or surroundings - You begin to avoid specific circumstances or environments. This avoidance might be motivated by the assumption that the event you're avoiding is the source of an initial panic attack. You may also avoid situations where getting aid would be difficult or impossible if you had a panic attack. When taken to its logical conclusion, phobic avoidance develops into agoraphobia.

The frequency, length, and intensity of panic episodes can all vary.

It is crucial to highlight that panic attacks are curable and effective methods and interventions for managing and overcoming them are available.

When should you see a doctor?

Consider seeing a healthcare professional, either your primary doctor or a therapist, if you are:

• struggling to get through the day and your symptoms are interfering with your relationships, work, or other daily activities;

• experiencing recurring physical symptoms, such as insomnia, heart palpitations, headaches, or any other form of pain; or

• using substances to cope with your anxiety and physical symptoms.

• having panic attacks after an injury or being

diagnosed with a medical condition;

• staying at home despite having responsibilities that require you to leave the house;

• wanting to understand your symptoms better or be screened for diagnosis;

• wanting to learn the best ways to self-manage your symptoms or the various treatment options for panic attacks.

Causes and Triggers of Panic Attacks

The precise origins of panic attacks are unknown, although they are thought to be a mix of biochemical, genetic, psychological, and environmental variables. Below are some of the most prominent causes and triggers of panic attacks:

10 Most Common Causes of Panic Attack

It might be tough to recognize what causes panic attacks if you suffer from anxiety. It might be tough to control your symptoms if a panic attack occurs for no apparent reason. That is why it is critical to recognize any anxiety triggers.

Stress

Stress is ranked first among the top ten panic attack triggers. Stress can be brought on by various factors, making it difficult to avoid. Work, school, family, health, and other factors can cause anxiety. As a common cause of panic attacks, practicing self-care and learning healthy coping mechanisms for stress management is critical. This may assist you in avoiding anxious symptoms.

Existing medical conditions

A health issue diagnosis can be unpleasant and stressful. Depending on the seriousness of your disease, you may be concerned about caring for your loved ones and being fit enough to work. A good diagnosis might quickly set off a panic attack. In this scenario, you may avoid panic attacks by contacting your doctor and following their advice.

Many drugs

Contraceptives, cold and flu drugs, and weight reduction pills can all trigger anxiety and panic. This is frequently due to the medication's adverse effects. A panic attack might be triggered by feeling physically ill. If you continue to have anxiety symptoms while taking certain drugs, talk to your doctor about possible alternatives.

Abuse of substances

Cocaine, methamphetamine, benzos, marijuana, and heroin can produce psychosis, including anxious symptoms. A panic attack is more likely to occur when someone is experiencing withdrawal symptoms. Co-occurring disorder treatment can address symptoms of both addiction and anxiety condition.

Caffeine

Coffee makes you more alert and raises your heart rate. In more severe circumstances, it might result in a panic attack. This can be prevented by replacing coffee or tea with non-caffeinated beverages.

Social gatherings

While we may occasionally feel uneasy in social circumstances, some people suffer from a social anxiety condition. You may feel overwhelmed if you are surrounded by a massive group of people or a lot of noise. Activities that need social engagement or introducing new individuals might set off a panic episode. You can always bring someone to these events if you're working on establishing appropriate coping mechanisms.

Reminders of horrific events

If you've had a terrible incident in the past, you may struggle with anything that reminds you of it.

Panic attacks can occur when confronted with exceptionally unpleasant or painful conditions. Anxiety is connected to post-traumatic stress disorder (PTSD), and those with symptoms of both conditions can benefit from PTSD therapy.

Diet

Food can have an impact on how your brain functions throughout the day. Eating protein and complex carbohydrates and drinking plenty of water can help you maintain your blood sugar levels and even increase serotonin levels. Serotonin has a relaxing impact on the brain, which can aid in preventing panic attacks. Getting your total eight hours of sleep every night is also critical.

Financial anxiety

Concerns about debt, bills, and finances may easily trigger anxiety. You can address this panic attack cause by consulting with a financial expert.

Feeling disorganized also contributes to financial worry, and an adviser may help you sort out your present circumstances and build a sound strategy.

Disagreements

A strained connection with a loved one or a heated quarrel is a classic cause of panic attacks. Disputes can be more distressing since you must actively attempt to resolve them. You're also frequently relying on the other side to reach an agreement or make reparations, which may give you the impression that you need more control over the issue. Speaking with a therapist and being open and honest with the other party might be beneficial.

It's crucial to note that not everyone who encounters these conditions will have panic attacks, and the reasons and triggers of panic attacks might differ from person to person. It's also worth noting that panic attacks can occur without an apparent cause or trigger, which is a spontaneous panic attack. If you have panic attacks, it's best to seek professional help from a professional mental health expert to determine what's causing them and build a treatment plan.

Separating Panic Attacks from Other Anxiety Disorders

Panic attacks are a form of anxiety illness characterized by brief and acute bouts of dread or discomfort. These are some crucial differences between panic attacks and other anxiety disorders:

1. Panic attacks vs. Generalized Anxiety Disorder (GAD): Panic attacks are brief and acute bouts of dread or discomfort. However, GAD is defined by persistent and excessive concern and anxiety about various ordinary circumstances or occurrences. GAD is characterized by the constant fear that is more widespread. In contrast, panic episodes are episodic and frequently accompanied by somatic symptoms such as a racing heart,

shortness of breath, and sweat.

2. Panic attacks vs. Social Anxiety Disorder: Social Anxiety Disorder, often known as social phobia, is characterized by acute anxiety about social or performance circumstances in which the individual is too concerned about being humiliated, criticized, or embarrassed. While panic attacks can occur in social events, they are not always initiated by them and can occur independently without any apparent trigger.

3. Particular phobias are excessive or unreasonable fears of certain items, circumstances, or activities, such as heights, spiders, flying, or needles. Specific phobias in some people can cause panic attacks, although not all panic attacks are, and panic attacks can occur without any discernible reason.

4. Panic attacks vs. Post-Traumatic Stress Disorder (PTSD): PTSD is an anxiety illness that can develop following a traumatic experience.

While panic attacks can occur in people who have PTSD, not all panic attacks are caused by a traumatic incident, and those who have the panic disorder may not have a history of trauma.

5. Panic attacks vs. Obsessive-Compulsive Disorder (OCD): Obsessive-Compulsive Disorder (OCD) is characterized by intrusive and repetitive thoughts (obsessions) and repetitive activities (compulsions) aimed at relieving anxiety.

While some people with OCD suffer anxiety or panic episodes, they are not a defining component of the disorder, and not all panic attacks are connected to OCD.

It's crucial to emphasize that a skilled mental health practitioner should accurately diagnose anxiety disorders, including panic disorders, based on a thorough review of symptoms, history, and specific circumstances. If you have anxiety or panic attacks, getting professional care for an accurate diagnosis and proper therapy is best.

Chapter 2

Managing Panic Attacks

Managing panic attacks consists of a variety of measures aimed at lowering the number and severity of panic attacks when they occur, and preventing them from interfering with everyday living. These are some successful panic attack management strategies:

Breathing exercises and relaxation techniques:

During a panic episode, deep breathing, progressive muscle relaxation, and other relaxation techniques can assist in calming the body and mind.

If you're having a panic attack and are breathing fast, completing a breathing exercise will help relieve your other symptoms. Consider this:

• *breathe in as slowly, deeply, and softly as you can through your nose*

•*breath out as slowly, thoroughly, and softly as*

you can via your mouth

• Some people find it beneficial to count from 1 to 5 on each in-breath and out-breath.

Within a few minutes, you should begin to feel better. You can feel exhausted afterward.

Cognitive-behavioral techniques: Cognitive-behavioral therapy (CBT) is a popular and effective treatment for panic disorder. CBT assists people in identifying and changing harmful thinking patterns and behaviors that lead to panic episodes. Identifying and challenging illogical beliefs, gaining coping strategies to control anxious thoughts, and eventually facing and desensitizing to trigger circumstances are examples.

Lifestyle changes: Keeping a healthy lifestyle might aid in managing panic attacks. Regular exercise, enough sleep, and a well-balanced diet can all assist in reducing stress and anxiety.

Avoiding coffee, alcohol, and nicotine, which can cause or worsen panic attacks in certain people, may also be beneficial.

Stress management: Practicing stress management practices such as mindfulness, meditation, or yoga can help reduce overall stress and minimize the likelihood of panic attacks.

Knowing the nature of panic attacks, their symptoms, and their causes can help individuals feel more empowered and less scared when having a panic attack.

Developing relaxation methods, coping skills, and self-care can also aid in managing panic episodes.

Establishing a network of sympathetic friends, family, or a therapist may give emotional support and encouragement during tough times. Communicating to trusted people about one's panic attacks might help minimize feelings of isolation while providing validation and understanding.

Medication can treat or alleviate some of the symptoms of panic disorder. It does not, however, treat or address the problem. Medication can be helpful in extreme situations, but it should not be the only option. Medicine is most successful when paired with other therapies that address the underlying causes of panic disorder, such as counseling and lifestyle modifications.

Antidepressants are one type of medication that may be utilized. Antidepressants take many weeks to start working, so you must take them continually, not only during a panic episode.

Benzodiazepines

These anti-anxiety medications work immediately (usually within 30 minutes to an hour). Taking them during a panic attack relieves symptoms quickly. Benzodiazepines, on the other hand, are highly addictive and have severe withdrawal symptoms; therefore, they should be taken cautiously.

Exposition therapy:

Under the supervision of a therapist, gradual exposure to trigger circumstances or activities that cause panic attacks might help desensitize patients to their concerns and lower the intensity of panic attacks over time. You may be asked to hyperventilate, move your head from side to side, or retain your breath. These various workouts produce sensations akin to panic episodes. With each exposure, you become less terrified of these internal physical feelings and gain more control over your panic attacks.

Self-help guidelines for panic attacks

No matter how helpless or out of control your panic attacks make you feel, it's crucial to realize that there are numerous things you can do to assist yourself. The following self-help approaches will significantly help you in overcoming panic:

Understand terror and anxiety

Merely learning more about panic attacks might help you feel better. Learn more about anxiety, panic disorder, and the fight-or-flight reaction during a panic attack. You'll realize that the emotions and sentiments you experience when you panic are normal and that you're not insane.

Avoid using tobacco, alcohol, and caffeine

They can all cause panic attacks in persons who are prone to them. Likewise, be cautious of stimulant-containing drugs, such as diet pills and non-drowsy cold treatments.

Discover how to regulate your breathing

Several of the feelings associated with a panic attack (such as lightheadedness and chest tightness) are exacerbated by hyperventilation. Deep breathing, on the other hand, can alleviate panic feelings. By learning to manage your breathing, you may calm yourself down when you feel stressed. You're also less likely to experience the emotions you're scared of if you know how to manage your breathing.

Use relaxing methods

When performed daily, yoga, meditation, and progressive muscle relaxation improve the body's relaxation response, which is the opposite of the stress reaction implicated in anxiety and panic. These relaxation methods improve ease and boost emotions of joy and serenity.

Make direct eye contact with relatives and friends.

Anxiety symptoms can worsen when you feel lonely, so contact individuals who care about you frequently. If you don't have someone to turn to, find methods to meet new individuals and form valuable connections.

Work out regularly

Exercise is a natural anxiety reducer, so aim to move for at least 30 minutes most days (three 10-minute sessions are just as good). Walking, jogging, swimming, or dancing, which need both your arms and legs to move, can be very beneficial.

Obtain adequate restorative sleep

Inadequate or low-quality sleep can exacerbate anxiety, so aim for seven to nine hours of undisturbed sleep every night.

It's crucial to remember that dealing with panic attacks may necessitate a combination of methods and approaches, and what works for one individual may not work for another. Working with a skilled professional in mental health to build a tailored treatment plan that meets one's unique requirements and circumstances is suggested. It is feasible to effectively manage panic attacks and enhance the overall quality of life with the proper support and management measures.

Helping Someone Who Is Having a Panic Attack

It can be terrifying to witness a friend or loved one having a panic attack. Their breathing may become fast and shallow, and they may feel dizzy or lightheaded, shake, sweat, feel sick, or suspect a heart attack. No matter how ridiculous you believe, their terrified reaction to a scenario is, keep in mind that the threat appears very real to your loved one. Just advising them to relax or downplaying their fears will not help. But, by assisting your loved one in surviving a panic attack, you might help them feel less scared of future episodes.

Maintain your cool

Being calm, empathetic, and nonjudgmental will aid in the relief of your loved one's terror.

Concentrate on your loved one's respiration. Locate a quiet area for him/her to sit, and then help them through a few minutes of calm, deep breathing.

Do physical activity

Raise and lower your arms or pound your feet together. It can assist in relieving some of your loved one's tension.

Pull them out of their thoughts by asking them to list five items around them or soothingly discussing a common interest.

Urge your loved one to get assistance

Your loved one may feel ashamed about experiencing a panic attack in front of you once the incident is ended. Assure them and urge them to seek anxiety treatment.

Chapter 3

Overcoming Panic Attacks

Overcoming panic attacks entails learning skills and techniques for effectively managing and reducing the frequency of panic episodes and progressively regaining control over one's thoughts, emotions, and behaviors.

Coping strategies for panic attacks

Because everyone experiences panic attacks differently, tactics that work for one person may not work for you. Specific tactics may work in one situation but not in another.

The goal is to experiment with different strategies to find the best ones.

1. Acknowledge that you are experiencing a panic attack.

When your symptoms begin, the first thing you can do is recognize them for what they are: a panic attack. It is not dangerous, will not hurt you, and will be gone shortly.

It may be tempting to flee from fear, but embracing your emotional condition might help you get through an episode.

Remind yourself that this is only a passing phase that will pass quickly.

2. Maintain your footing

Many panic attack sufferers find it beneficial to ground themselves in their surroundings. Remaining in the present moment might help alleviate unreality and terror emotions.

There are several strategies for staying grounded.

The 5-4-3-2-1 technique is one of them. It entails focusing on your five senses to help you connect with your environment.

The 5-4-3-2-1 technique works as follows:

• 5: Name FIVE objects you notice around you.

• 4: Identify FOUR objects around you that you can touch.

- 3: Identify THREE items you can hear.

- 2: Name TWO things you can smell.

- 1: Identify ONE item you can taste.

Some people find that smelling lavender helps them stay grounded, and studies have shown that breathing this perfume can lessen anxiety.

Do you want to try any more grounding techniques?

- Firmly press your feet into the ground.

- Consume one of your favorite dishes or beverages (for added benefit, do it mindfully).

- Keep a journal to record your emotions.

- Locate and concentrate on your pulse.

3. Let your muscles relax

Muscle relaxation methods can provide several health advantages, including:

- decrease blood pressure

- improve sleep

- reduce anxiety.

Relaxing techniques such as progressive muscle relaxation can help alleviate anxiety.

Muscle relaxation techniques alleviate stress by tightening and progressively relaxing muscles, reducing tension throughout the body. You can tension your muscles for 5 to 10 seconds or as long as you feel comfortable.

How to go about it:

- Begin by sitting or lying down in a relaxed position. Shut your eyes for a moment.

- Take a deep breath, observing how the air fills your lungs. Hold your breath for a few seconds before releasing it.

- Take another big breath, hold it, and then slowly exhale.

- Begin with your feet. Curl your toes and arch your feet to tense your feet. Hold for a few seconds, then relax your feet.

- Contract the calves' muscles. Hold it for a few seconds, then let go.

- Continue by pressing your thighs together. Hold, then let go.

- Contract your stomach and chest muscles. Suck it in, squeeze it, and hold it. Then relax, allowing your body to go limp.

- Tighten your back muscles by drawing your shoulders together. Hold, then let go.

- Switch to your arms. Form a fist and compress your entire arm. Hold it for a few seconds, then let go.

- Tighten the muscles in your neck, face, and head. Hold it for a few seconds, then let go.

- Lastly, stiffen your entire body at the same time. Squeeze harder, hold it, and then let go.

- Move your muscles slowly to wake them up. Shake it all up. When you're ready, stretch and open your eyes.

4. *Exercise mindfulness*

Being mindful entails being aware, remaining present, and embracing how you feel in the current time.

You may alleviate the discomfort caused by a panic attack by expressing how you feel emotionally and physically without judgment. You may accept and reflect on your symptoms rather than become angry and terrified.

According to a reliable source, mindfulness-based therapies are as helpful as cognitive behavioral therapy (CBT) in reducing anxiety. Of course, the benefits will vary depending on the individual.

Practicing mindfulness may be highly beneficial if uncomfortable physiological sensations frequently trigger your panic episodes. Accepting nonthreatening bodily emotions rather than fighting them can help prevent panic attacks.

Mindfulness techniques include meditation,

yoga, and breathing exercises.

5. *Imagine your happy place.*

It may seem obvious, but visualizing yourself in a happy place or surrounded by people who care about you can provide immense comfort during a panic attack.

Try having a photo of individuals or places that make you happy on hand.

6. *Speak with someone*

Talking to someone who provides comfort is far better than imagining them. They can not only bring a required sense of security and delight but also remind you that your symptoms are only temporary and will not harm you.

Sometimes all you need is a friend or family member to hold your hand or distract you with talk when you are under attack.

7. *Be patient.*

Another option is to ride through the panic episode. Although it may appear contradictory, embracing your anxiety rather than avoiding it might help panic attacks pass more quickly and prevent them in the future.

You can regain control if you demonstrate that you can feel all these overwhelming symptoms and emerge safe and well.

8. *Recognize your triggers*

Panic attacks can appear out of nowhere. But, in many situations, there are subtle underlying causes for fear.

Identifying the source of your panic episodes is a key step in managing them. Understanding your triggers is particularly beneficial in psychotherapy.

Though it may take some time, maintaining a journal to reflect on previous panic attacks will assist you in determining trends and causes.

The idea isn't to avoid the triggers but to learn how to deal with and confront them.

9. Create a plan.

Preparing for a panic attack entails learning what to expect and why they occur. If you've already had a panic attack, you probably know what worked and what didn't. Did breathing exercises improve or aggravate your symptoms? What about physical activity?

Making a plan and thinking about these things will help you feel more in control and minimize the intensity of future panic episodes.

10. Control your stress

Stress management is one of the most effective techniques to treat panic episodes and enhance general well-being.

Treatment strategies will differ from person to person; some people will use medications to control their symptoms, while others will attend frequent treatment. Others may discover that relaxation and self-care techniques might help them manage their panic episodes.

It's a bit of everything sometimes, but stress management can benefit everyone.

Breathing techniques, meditation, keeping a diary, and spending time in nature are all strategies for stress management.

11. Workout

The effects of exercise on anxiety and panic levels differ from person to person.

According to research, regular exercise can help reduce stress and anxiety and enhance sleep quality and mood.

Because exercise can elevate your heart rate, cause you to sweat, and have other side effects that mirror panic, you should start with more modest exercise if it causes a panic attack.

Additionally, to assist in managing your stress

and anxiety, try a new fitness program or activity you love, such as yoga or walking.

12. Take your medicine as directed

If you have been prescribed medicine by a healthcare practitioner, you must take it as directed. You may always contact them if you have any concerns regarding side effects or wish to make changes.

13. Confront negative beliefs

CBT is a commonly used and generally rated treatment for panic and other anxiety disorders.

Individuals who suffer from panic attacks usually have negative and fear-based mental processes, which can lead to or worsen worry.

CBT seeks to replace distorted and harmful thinking with more rational and accurate thinking.

CBT approaches can also help you develop coping strategies and make adjustments to manage panic and anxiety better.

14. Experiment with exposure treatment.

Exposure therapy entails exposing yourself to whatever causes your panic episodes or anxieties.

Exposing yourself to your triggers may appear frightening and counterproductive. But, continually understanding that these experiences will not harm you can make a difference in the long term.

A mental health practitioner should always initiate exposure treatment.

15. Consult a physician

If you or a loved one has been experiencing panic attacks, you can seek help from a healthcare expert.

If you don't have access to a healthcare professional, consider looking into the health services or contacting a local clinic.

Complications from panic attacks

If untreated, panic attacks and panic disorders may influence practically every part of your life. You may be so frightened of experiencing additional panic attacks that you live in a continual state of terror, destroying your quality of life.

Problems that panic attacks may cause or be connected to include:

• Development of particular phobias, such as dread of driving or leaving your home

• Frequent medical treatment for health issues and other medical conditions

• Avoidance of social situations

• Problems at work or school

• Depression, anxiety disorders, and other mental illnesses

• Increased risk of suicide or suicidal thoughts

• Alcohol or other substance misuse

• Financial concerns

For some people, panic disorder may entail agoraphobia avoiding locations or circumstances that cause distress because you fear being unable to flee or find treatment if you have a panic attack. Alternatively, you may depend on people to be with you to leave your house.

Conclusion

Finally, congrats on finishing "No Need to Panic: A Guide to Managing and Overcoming Panic Attacks. I hope you found this book's information, strategies, and tools helpful in your journey to manage and overcome panic attacks.

Remember that dealing with panic attacks takes time, effort, and practice. Being patient with yourself and recognizing and enjoying your tiny victories is critical. Recovering from panic attacks can be difficult, but with dedication, strength, and the appropriate tactics, you can restore control of your life.

Continue to emphasize self-care, practice coping methods, and confront negative thinking patterns as you progress. Use the aid of your loved ones and, if necessary, seek expert help. Remember that it is OK to seek assistance when necessary.

I invite you to return to the book's chapters and

activities as required and to modify the tactics to your specific needs and situations. Every person's experience is unique, and figuring out what works best for you is critical.

Remember that your panic episodes do not define you. You are capable of living an entire life apart from terror. You can flourish and create a future free of panic episodes with focus, self-compassion, and tenacity.

I wish you all the best as you manage and overcome panic episodes. You can reclaim control of your life and live it with hope, resilience, and joy. You can do it!

9 798391 234326